Production by AL!TE
Bourne Park
Cores End Road
Bourne End SL8 5AS

© **Alistair Smith 2001**
ISBN: 1-85539-089-2

First published 2001
Reprinted 2003

Published by: Network Educational Press Ltd
www.networkpress.co.uk

Design and layout: Neil Hawkins

Edited by: Carol Thompson and Debbie Pullinger

Printed in Great Britain by: MPG Books Ltd

visit the website www.alite.co.uk

LEADING LEARNING

Contents

	an introduction
Section 1	changing trends
Section 2	attitudes to learning
Section 3	the neurological basis of learning
Section 4	understanding memory
Section 5	music and learning
Section 6	stress
Section 7	the physiology of learning
Section 8	engagement and motivation
Section 9	connectivity
Section 10	effective learning strategies
Section 11	effective questioning strategies
Section 12	target setting
Section 13	formative assessment
Section 14	preparing for exams
Section 15	thinking skills
Section 16	models of intelligence
Section 17	staff development

an introduction

This book of posters for leading learning and transforming teaching derives from the many hundreds of workshops on learning and teaching which I have delivered in recent years.

The texts come from different sources. Some are observations about learning, based on my own work and put into sayings; some are from researchers in different academic disciplines; and some come from research on social and economic trends. It is intended that the posters can be used in educational establishments to bolster staff development and to test and challenge thinking about the scope and purpose of learning.

These posters are in copyright and their use is confined to within the purchasing establishment. However, I would hope that educationalists can be creative in the use of the poster material, a key purpose of which is to lead learners into learning. Take the thoughts described within these pages and use them to bemuse, challenge, inform and extend your colleagues.

Every effort has been made to identify the source of the poster material. Where there is no source stated then the material is my own.

The term *kaizen* may be familiar to you if you have been involved in management training or if you have read any organizational development literature. *Kaizen* is the Japanese concept of organizational change which authorizes and values small, almost imperceptible, ongoing and never-ending improvements. Little things accrue great value in *kaizen*. Small keys open big doors.

In schools and colleges and in classrooms generally, 'don't denizem their *kaizen*' is a good maxim. I was astonished recently to hear from a headteacher who was lamenting a consequence of a reducing budget – that staff tea and coffee, previously free and unlimited over breaks, was now to be stopped. As I listened to this tale unfold I thought of the consequence of removing something which is seemingly trivial to an accountant or a tax payer but which may have a different set of meanings for a member of staff. The headteacher was guilty of 'denizem their *kaizen*' and the impact on morale, willingness to give that extra yard, sense of common purpose, and daily opportunities for social cohesion, was diminished in a small but perceptible way which would not be recovered by a simple reversal of the decision. Small things add up. The posters provided in this book, although slight in appearance, can be heavy in consequence and are part of your *kaizen* repertoire. Their use can signify greater changes.

Kaizen, small incremental and never-ending improvements, are of no use if you and your organization are 'in confuzen'. An organization 'in confuzen' has not agreed and set its priorities; it has not got a direction and a sense of purpose and is not focused on what matters. An organization such as a school or college 'in confuzen' is wasting its time with *kaizen*.

How does an organization decide what is important and begin to accommodate all the trivia with all the other big challenges that come along? What, if anything, should get lost along the way? Is staffroom tea and coffee more important than a bullying policy or new windows for the science block or the child who's experimenting with drugs? How is it possible to do it all? Is it advisable to even try?

Charles Handy, a management guru much favoured in the UK, uses lots of analogies for management and prioritization. He would wish any organization to be clear about core purpose and not to lose sight of delivering that core purpose. He would want your school to focus on the core stuff. He uses this analogy to help explain his prioritization philosophy.

How do you get rocks, stones, pebbles, sand and water into a small glass jar? Pile it all in at once and it overflows. Sand and water will fill it almost to the brim anyway. Grinding the lot down by brute force and sheer will power may be one method, but it leaves a mess and some damage along the way. The answer? Sort out the big stuff first.

Put your rocks in early. Lodge them in place, then build the other materials around what is solid, unquestionable and commonly agreed-on as more important than anything else. This is the equivalent of focusing unerringly on the learner and the quality of the learning experience at all times in your school or college. All educational establishments claim to do this. Few really do. For most it's the manic dance of putting in one set of rocks then swapping them around, filling up with pebbles then taking some out again. A visitor, an 'expert', an official or an inspector arrives with new rocks, stones, pebbles, sand and water and before you know it the jar is being emptied again. A rock edict arrives in a brown envelope: the definition of a rock is changed! Academic research shows that what we thought were rocks are not in fact authentic rocks. Statisticians show that rocks are not what they used to be. Higher-order rocks are what is required. Rock measurements are discredited. You just can't get the sand nowadays! In the midst of all of this, what certainties prevail?

The certainties which prevail hang around our core purpose of 'leading learners to learn'. That's where *kaizen* comes in. That's where the posters come in. All the posters in this book are concerned with the issues of learning and with how to lead learners to learn. When you have secured clarity about core purpose; when that core purpose is expressed at the levels of vision, mission, goals, targets and tasks; when everyone knows what is expected of them, to what level, with what resource and against what measures, then you put in the stones, the pebbles, the sand and the water. The *kaizen* or small things are the stones, the pebbles, the sand and the water. You can only get them in and to best effect when the big stuff is secure.

Two tenets of effective staff development for schools are that coaching on the job is the most effective mechanism for sustained teaching improvement and that programmes, not events, are better for securing such improvements. Again, this may depend on the rocks being in place. If you do not have a view of what is good teaching and what is effective learning, and have colleagues who consistently exhibit the former and reflect on the latter, then it is hard to coach for it. If you do not have clarity of vision about how you wish to secure good teaching and, effective learning, then it is impossible to plan a sustaining support programme for it. You need the rocks and, what's more, they need to be your own rocks! Inspectorate, local authority officers, prospective parents and the occasional politician may, from time-to-time, come and look at your rocks; they may even offer you their own, but yours are best. Avoid accepting someone else's definitions of good teaching and effective learning. Invariably such definitions are circumscribed by precedent and by the circumstances which generated them. Definitions of teaching which arise from observed experience of what has gone before can take you to a very dull place: a place where mediocrity can be rewarded. Similarly, in a world where children communicate as readily by word of mouse as by word of mouth, fresh thinking about the timing, the scope, the site and the methodology of learning is overdue.

Time spent on learning about learning is part of your professional responsibility. The posters in this book can enhance this process; they can assist in your coaching and mentoring programmes and they can be part of your attempts to capture and sustain freshness in approaches to teaching and thinking about learning.

The posters can be used as part of the induction programme for new and supply staff and as part of your support for teachers in training. The simple expedient of a focus for the week or fortnight, derived from one of the poster sources and shared at staff briefing and later debriefing, can have as much effect as a conference. The relevant poster(s) can then be reduced and put in the staff briefing sheet or enlarged and put on a staff notice board to prompt further discussion. For example, primacy and recency – positive beginnings and endings to lessons – could be a two-week focus.

The staff handbook can contain excerpts from the poster collection. Poster packs can be made available for departmental meetings. Some posters are appropriate for themed assemblies, for display in classrooms or around the school or college generally. The messages can be used as screen savers on the computer network, as a theme of the week on the school or college website or as part of the closed-circuit televised message system. Some poster material may be suited to parents' evenings or for presentations to governing bodies. Some can be used, albeit judiciously, for staff development within the school or college.

Each poster offers the possibility of a small, almost imperceptible, ongoing and never-ending improvement – and as such is your *kaizen*.

Alistair Smith January 2001

LEADING
LEARNING

'In a changing world,
5 dispositions are worth
securing:

resilience
responsibility
resourcefulness
reasoning
reflectivity-reflexivity.'

'There are now more computers in a 5-series BMW than were used in any of the Apollo missions into space.'

Changing Trends

'In the UK we have a very good and well-managed school system, we just don't have a very good education system.'

'There is a direct link between education and improved earning potential. According to the Royal Economic Society's research with identical twins, published in July 2000, each extra year in education yielded an extra 8% increase in pay.'

Changing Trends

'In an April 2000 MORI poll carried out for the UK Campaign for Learning, 56% of the 2,600 14–16 year olds interviewed, reported that what they spent most time doing in class was copying from the board or from a book.'

Campaign for Learning, Learning to Learn Project, 2000

'The country is going through a big transition from an industrial economy to a knowledge economy.
Education is the key mechanism to get through efficiently and beat the international competition.'

Professor David Hargreaves, QCA, November 2000

'65% of children polled said they would like to do well in school,

45% thought they would,

35% of their teachers thought they would.'

Professor John MacBeath, 1999
University of Cambridge

Changing Trends

'In an information age, you can chase content but you can never catch it – chase the learning dispositions instead.'

'The cost to a bank of handling a customer transaction over the internet is 1p, compared to 10p over the phone and £1 face to face.'

'The average family has 22 fewer hours each week to spend at home than families had 30 years ago.'

Changing Trends

'If it hadn't been for my teacher who got me into rowing, I wouldn't be here now.'

Sir Steven Redgrave, Olympic gold medal winner, interviewed after winning his fifth

visit the website   www.alite.co.uk

Attitudes to Learning

'I think everyone has genius within them. If every teacher in every school treated every child as a potential genius, what do you think the effect would be?
If you tell somebody they can do something,
give them some belief, their expectation goes up.'

© David Hockney

Attitudes to Learning

'It's not how many answers students know, it's how they behave when they don't know that counts.'

Professor Arthur Costa, Institute of Intelligence

'We don't
see things the
way they are,
we see things
the way we are.'

Anaïs Nin, author

Attitudes to Learning

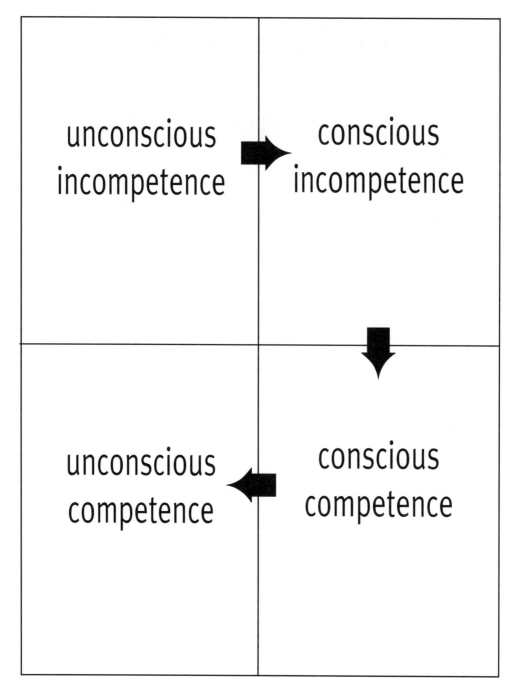

unconscious
incompetence

conscious
incompetence

unconscious
competence

conscious
competence

visit the website   www.alite.co.uk

Attitudes to Learning

'Teachers' perceptions of a pupil's intelligence strongly affect the pupil's own view of his or her ability, and pupils' opinions of peers are heavily influenced by such perceptions.'

Deborah Eyre, Deputy Head of
Westminster Institute of Education

Attitudes to Learning

'In survey after survey students tell us they are not challenged by school.'

Attitudes to Learning

LEADING
LEARNING

'Your belief in your ability shapes your ability.'

Attitudes to Learning

'You can tell the good teachers because they never shout, they smile and make you laugh, they know your name and they never give you work you can't do.'

Year 8 pupil, Bristol

'I remember an experienced member of staff, who never ever had trouble with a pupil with whom the rest of us struggled, telling me his secret: unobserved tokens of kindness! He found out that this boy had an interest in fishing and he would bring him in old copies of the fishing magazines his brother-in-law bought. He then slipped them quietly to the boy without making a fuss. I suppose if you surprise someone with kindness, they can't resist you after that.'

Teacher contributing to a behaviour management session

'Neural plasticity offers you the chance to become unique – you are not the person you were a minute ago.'

Susan Greenfield
Professor of Pharmacology and
Director of the Royal Institution of Pharmacology

visit the website www.alite.co.uk

The Neurological Basis of Learning

'Mice that had exercised on a wheel had more BDNF (brain-derived growth factor) which enhances the ability of neurons to connect with one another. Mouse learning also improved with short periods of rest.'

visit the website www.alite.co.uk

The Neurological Basis of Learning

'Constructive reflection is important in that it allows the brain's frontal lobe region a chance to filter information and draw associations with prior learning.'

Frydenberg and Lewis,
British Journal of Educational Psychology, 1999

visit the website www.alite.co.uk

The Neurological Basis of Learning

'People who drink heavily for thirty to forty years die with brains that weigh 105 grams less than the brains of their light drinking friends. Alcoholics and heavy drinkers kill off about 60,000 more neurons than light drinkers. Studies of the brains of alcoholic men showed reduced blood flow in the frontal lobe, the seat of memory formation, creativity and problem solving. Alcohol also suppresses REM sleep which affects memory consolidation. In women and children these effects are exaggerated.'

Dr Pierce J Howard, *The Owner's Manual for the Brain*, Bard Press, 1994

'In recent research led by UC London it was shown that those areas of the brain contributing to visual and spatial orientation were significantly more developed in London taxi drivers than in the general population.'

'Visualizing the activity fires the same neural circuitry as undertaking the visualized activity and thus modifies the brain.'

The Neurological Basis of Learning

'Focused attention directed at visual stimuli cancels out the suppressive influence of competing stimuli.'

Dr Leslie Ungerleider

visit the website   www.alite.co.uk

'From fruit flies to humans, distributed learning works better than amassed learning and so adding more content comes at a price.'

The Neurological Basis of Learning

'The hippocampal and visual cortex areas of a child's brain are activated when the child is listening to a story. Powerful stories elicit long-term visual memories.'

Dr Martha Farah, 'The neural basis of mental imagery', *The Cognitive Neurosciences*, 1995, pp.963-75, The MIT Press

'We know there's a part of the brain… that gets activated when we're very emotional, and it increases our ability to remember things. When there's emotion attached to something we're more likely to remember it.'

Dr Marilyn Albert, Professor of Psychology,
Harvard Medical School

The Neurological Basis of Learning

'Adolescent exposure to nicotine contributes to subsequent and permanent behavioural problems – especially for females. A possible explanation is that nicotine retards cell division in the hippocampus, an area which continues growing into adulthood in females but not in males.

Nicotine also acted as a suppressant and reduced the amounts of dopamine and norepinephrine produced. These chemicals are lower in humans who are suffering from depression. Some studies suggest that starting to smoke early on in life can increase the chances of suffering depression in adulthood.'

Duke University, USA, published in *Brain Research*, October 2000

'Let the children you teach know that through the choices exercised now they select the sort of brain they end up with for life.

Substance or alcohol abuse, early and extended exposure to nicotine, lack of exercise and a poor diet all have damaging effects on the brain.

Such effects can be permanent. They are most likely to occur in the brain's immature phase.
The immature phase extends from minus 9 months to about 24 years!'

The Neurological Basis of Learning

'The brain you have in your teenage years is not the one you end up with as an adult!'

The Neurological Basis of Learning

'Memory is the potential for connections to be made.'

Susan Greenfield, Professor of Pharmacology and
Director of the Royal Institution

'Trying to learn without reviewing is like trying to fill the bath without putting the plug in.'

Mike Hughes , *Closing The Learning Gap*,
Network Educational Press, 1999

visit the website www.alite.co.uk

Memory and the brain

* there is no one 'place' where memory resides – certain regions are specialized for storing certain components

* memory is a reconstructive process and as time passes memories change as the brain changes

* rehearsal is something the brain likes and there may be specialized circuitry for mimicry

* as you become expert, the activation levels in the brain go down

visit the website   www.alite.co.uk

'Constructive reflection is important in that it allows the brain's frontal lobe region a chance to filter information and draw associations with prior learning.'

Frydenberg and Lewis,
British Journal of Educational Psychology, 1999

Understanding Memory

'At the neurological level, memory storage is the alteration of the probability of a neural network firing in the future.'

Professor Daniel Schacter, *Searching for Memory*, Basic Books, 1997

Understanding Memory

We retain:

* 10% of what we read

* 20% of what we hear

* 30% of what we see

* 50% of what we hear and see

* 70% of what we say

* 90% of what we say and do

Source unknown

'Through reflectivity the brain becomes reflexive. In other words, genuine learning occurs with space for review.'

'As you get older three things happen to you. First of all your memory goes... and I can't remember the other two.'

Sir Norman Wisdom OBE
on receiving his knighthood, aged 84

'IQ has no impact on exam success. Memory is the key to good GCSE results.'

Headline, *Times Educational Supplement*, 18 June 1999

'I can remember the look of that classroom as though it were yesterday.'

Understanding Memory

Put on your memory specs:

See it

Personalize it

Exaggerate it

Connect it

Share it

'Our capacity to store and recall visual and spatial information is phenomenal.'

'Training a child in music at three or four years of age improves the way in which their brain develops patterns in space and time.'

Professor Gordon Shaw,
UC Irvine and co-originator of the
'Mozart effect' research

Music and the brain

* larger corpus callosum in adult musicians

* primary motor-cortex and the cerebellum larger

* musically trained adults perform better on word tests

* infants who have taken piano lessons for six months perform better on puzzle solving

* Seven year olds who have taken piano lessons and played computer maths games do better on maths tests than those who have played computer maths games but have taken extra reading instead of piano

visit the website www.alite.co.uk

'Brain scans taken during musical performances show that virtually the entire cerebral cortex is active while musicians are playing.'

Music can impact on learning in any combination of the following ways:

*   it can act as a carrier for content

*   it can energize or relax

*   it can prime performance

*   it can improve phonological awareness

visit the website   www.alite.co.uk

'All over the world, mothers pick up their infants and babble with them. Are we programmed to do this?'

Music and Learning

'Undergraduates in a control group, undertaking mathematical tasks involving spatial and rotational symmetry, showed significant performance improvements when played Mozart's *Piano Sonata for two Pianos in D*, for 10 minutes prior to the task.'

visit the website www.alite.co.uk

'I use music during some science discussion group activities.

When I lower the volume of the music the noise in the class goes down.'

Teacher, Stirling, Scotland

Music and Learning

'baroque-a-bye baby'

Advertisement for a boxed CD set of
Mozart piano pieces intended to make
your infant super-intelligent

'A child who can spend the day singing the lyrics of an entire pop album gives a clue as to how she might remember obscure and sometimes disconnected information.'

Music and Learning

'We all have default behavioural modes, to which we instinctively resort when threat becomes overwhelming. A teacher may resort to teaching how he or she was taught, with all the implicit risks therein.'

'Stress has its uses if you are a zebra on the savannah, and a lion's on the loose. It's not so useful when it comes with the bottom set last two periods on a wet Friday in November.'

Stress

'I make a distinction between challenge and stress. Challenge helps learning. Stress arises when we experience helplessness and a loss of control. It ultimately stops any learning.'

'A stressor is anything from the outside world which tips us out of homeostatic balance. The stress response is anything we do to retain homeostatic balance.'

Stress

'When challenge tips into stress you will see fight, flight, freeze and flock behaviours.'

'Stress in a classroom arises from threat – perceived or real.'

Stress

'We can turn on the stress response by thought and if you turn it on chronically, you are going to get sick.'

Professor Robert Sapolsky, *Why Zebras Don't Get Ulcers*, The MIT Press, 1999

10 classroom stressors:

* low self-esteem
* lack of self-belief
* unpredictability
* unacceptable levels of risk
* feeling out of control
* inability to make connections
* lack of perceived worth
* negative, or no, feedback
* poor communications
* inappropriate learning diet

LEADING
LEARNING

'Under stress, the indexing capacities of the brain are reduced, and the brain's short-term memory, and ability to form permanent new memories, are inhibited.'

Stress

'Don't wait until the flocking instinct is complicated by hormones – use structured and teacher-directed groupings from day one.'

Stress

'Too hot, too cold,

too hungry,

too tired

or too still...

and forget about

learning.'

'Children's memory, problem-solving abilities and reaction times are all adversely affected by lack of, or the wrong sort of, breakfast.'

'We are none of us very good at sitting still for extended periods of time with our attentional systems all engaged by one set of stimuli.'

The Physiology of Learning

'Learning and memory are consolidated during the REM and slow-wave sleep phases.'

'As adults we need the equivalent of 1.8 litres of water a day to preserve the electrolyte balance in the brain and to alleviate inattention and drowsiness.'

visit the website www.alite.co.uk

The Physiology of Learning

'Humour and play tap in to the primal need to imitate and mimic, as well as allowing us to make mistakes without dire consequences.'

The Physiology of Learning

'Laughter increases our immunity to illness, improves sleep, enhances neural growth, and results in tests of problem-solving ability improve when preceded by laughter.'

Dr Pierce J Howard, Director of Research,
Centre for Applied Cognitive Studies, NC, USA

The Physiology of Learning

'Adults laugh up to
twenty times a day,
while young children
laugh as much as
three hundred times.'

Dr Pierce J Howard, Director of Research,
Centre for Applied Cognitive Studies, NC, USA

'One of the greatest hindrances to learning is the notion, inherited from the eighteenth century, that mind and body are separate.'

'Movement, when part of learning, can provide reprieve from physical stress, enhance fine and large motor-movement, improve co-ordination and laterality, and link to learning.'

'Every physical state has its own library of memories, and states are the only thing we pay money for.'

Eric Jensen, *Teaching with the Brain in Mind*, Association for Supervision and Curriculum Development (ASCD), Virginia, USA, 1998

'Motion and e-motion: the two forgotten secrets of learning.'

The Physiology of Learning

'Get it into the muscle and it resists forgetting.'

'Most misbehaviour in classrooms is about movement.'

Professor Robert Sylwester, *A Celebration of Neurons: An Educator's Guide to the Human Brain*, Association for Supervision and Curriculum Development (ASCD), 1995

visit the website www.alite.co.uk

'With some types of dementia, memory of physically rehearsed movement seems to go last.'

'Teaching science has never been the same since we discovered modelling! Organizing competing teams of pupils into different atoms and then looking at ways in which they could combine, gave us lots of memorable experiences to which we could connect learning. Once you've role-played intimacy with another atom of chlorine you don't forget it in a hurry!'

Science teacher, Newcastle

The Physiology of Learning

'You can use brain-break exercises to improve handwriting, understanding of shapes and symbols, familiarity with letters and numbers, balance, motor control and ability to give focused attention.'

'If you think about it hard enough, there are great opportunities within literacy and numeracy to represent key understanding through physical movements. The movements can be large or small, individual or team, seated or in space to move around.'

Secondary teacher, Redruth, Cornwall

The Physiology of Learning

'To enrol learners in meaningful learning, take them with you to the edge of their comfort zone, but do so in small, clearly signalled steps.
Don't make challenge overwhelming.'

'All meaningful lifelong learning involves risk.'

Engagement and Motivation

'In a 1999 survey of 1,400 13–19-year-old boys in the UK, self-esteem was found to be the key to determining their future. How they felt about themselves affected friendships, their approach to the new and unknown and whether they were prepared to take the risk of learning, which involved revealing ignorance or making mistakes.'

A Katz, A Buchanan & A McCoy,
'Leading Lads' survey, 1999

(Research carried out by Oxford University, Department of Applied Social Policy and Social Research in association with Young Voice)

'In very general terms, the younger the child, the fewer the chunks of novel and dissociated information they can hold.

Use these guidelines when presenting steps to follow, class rules or factual information for the first time:

3–7	years	up to 3 chunks
7–10	years	3-plus chunks
10–14	years	5 chunks
14–16	years	5-plus chunks
16-plus		7 chunks

Model chunking in class.
Help children practise at home.'

‘The best strategy for esteeming learners is to involve them more in their own learning.’

'The basics of self-esteem are: belonging, aspiration, safety, identity, challenge, success.'

'You will experience the motivation show on two frequencies:

WII-FM and MMFI-AM

Radio What's In It For Me?

and

Radio Make Me Feel It's All Meaningful.'

'You cannot teach self-esteem. You can esteem the learner; you can provide "esteeming" experiences and you can equip the learner with tools to reframe their experiences more positively. Those are the limits of your influence.'

Engagement and Motivation

'A study of 15 global companies attributes 85–90% of leadership success to emotional intelligence. At the highest levels, EI accounts for virtually the entire advantage.'

Chris Dyson, Hay Group, UK, 2000

LEADING LEARNING

'The skills
of positive visualization
and
mental rehearsal of
patterns of success
are
vital to any top
performer and can be
taught.'

Engagement and Motivation

'The most mature person in any social setting is the one who is most adaptable to other people's needs.'

John Dewey

'Intellect cannot work at its best without emotional intelligence.'

Daniel Goleman, *Emotional Intelligence*,
Bloomsbury, 1995

'We allow ourselves to learn when we feel engaged and can readily connect to what we deem valuable.'

Connectivity

'You only understand information relative to what you already understand.'

Connectivity

'The To Do list is a good way of making connections explicit. At the end of the day, write three simple connecting tasks on the board, to be begun and completed first thing the next morning.'

'Encourage connective thinking by using comparisons. In marking and in target-setting, use previous efforts as a baseline for improvements.'

Connectivity

'The life map that we put up on the classroom wall helped me see the point of what we were doing.'

Year 5 pupil who completed a life-mapping exercise and put his map with the others on the 'aspirational wall'

'Give analogies, examples and case studies which, by their nature, connect. Make comparisons with tangible phenomena from their world.'

Connectivity

'Do your pupils have a clue as to why they are learning what they are learning – have you told them?'

'Information is not knowledge.'

Susan Greenfield, Professor of Pharmacology and
Director of the Royal Institution

Connectivity

'All children learn best when they are helped to understand the underlying principles for themselves.'

LEADING
LEARNING

'Failure
to connect
is
failure
to learn.'

Connectivity

7 things to avoid at the start of lessons:

* the prophecy of doom

* the generalized threat

* isolation of failure

* weary resignation

* a promise you can't keep

* leaky boiler (Shhh...)

* 'I'm waiting'

Effective Learning Strategies

'A positive start includes a relaxed but purposeful atmosphere, clear signalling of outcomes and clarity about working methods.'

Effective Learning Strategies

'Begin with
preview–review
and
end with
review–preview.'

Effective Learning Strategies

'All cultures
give significance
to
beginnings
and
endings.'

Effective Learning Strategies

'Go back to your embedded questions throughout the lesson – have we answered this question yet?'

Effective Learning Strategies

LEADING
LEARNING

'In tests of recall, adults consistently remembered items at the beginning and at the ending of the list.'

Effective Learning Strategies

'Top and tail tasks
with review–preview;
make those tasks
language-rich;
challenge through
questions;
structure with
diversity.'

Effective Learning Strategies

'Use time to shape and define the learning challenge, not to bolster sanctions.'

Effective Learning Strategies

For effective classroom practice, VAKplus

*   Visual

*   Auditory

*   Kinesthetic

    plus. . .

compelling questions throughout.

Effective Learning Strategies

'Connect

preview

focus on task

diffuse

focus on task

diffuse

focus on task

diffuse

review.'

Effective Learning Strategies

LEADING LEARNING

'Whatever your subject, whoever your group, whenever your lesson, VAKplus will enhance the learning.'

Effective Learning Strategies

'Regular participative review within lessons, and space for collective review at the end, is the best classroom intervention to keep recall high.'

Effective Learning Strategies

11 ways to group:

* mixed-ability
* mixed-role
* single sex
* boy-girl-boy-girl
* pre-designated
* inividual-pair-share-present
* carousel by activity
* snowball by information
* circle
* home groups for discussion
* away groups for activity

Effective Learning Strategies

'Focus and
diffuse
to optimize
engagement
with
learning.'

Effective Learning Strategies

'Manage
attentional
states,
not
just time
or
activity.'

visit the website   www.alite.co.uk

Effective Learning Strategies

LEADING
LEARNING

'One of the biggest influences
on classroom learning
is the amount of
structured and
purposeful
learner-talk the teacher
can initiate.'

Effective Learning Strategies

'Your own examples,
case studies and stories
enliven learning and are
remembered.
Time them like this:

your story 60%
your point 20%
your link to learning 20%.'

Adapted from Dale Carnegie,
with thanks to Glen Capelli

LEADING LEARNING

'The greatest enemy of learning is coverage. As long as you are determined to cover everything you guarantee that most kids are not going to understand.'

Howard Gardner, Professor of Education and Adjunct Professor of Neuroscience, Harvard

Effective Learning Strategies

'With groupings, play home and away – home groups are friendship-oriented and are safe; away groups are teacher-directed and involve some risk.'

Effective Learning Strategies

'Make the need for, and the rules for, structured variety in group-work explicit to pupils from the outset.'

Effective Learning Strategies

'To activate
real understanding,
represent the key
learning via the
different
intelligences.'

'The simplest and most effective audit for your classroom practice is VAKplus: in what ways can I convey this information through seeing, hearing and doing while optimizing the use of questions throughout?'

'Perform
your
understanding
to
show you
know.'

'I hear and
I forget;
I see and
I remember;
I do and
I understand.'

Ancient Chinese proverb

Effective Learning Strategies

'In classroom instruction, write the outcomes you seek, the questions to be answered and the key terminology above eye level and to the left of the board.'

'We did away with bells, put auxiliary whiteboards for lesson objectives in the main focal space in each room, and filled the available classroom and corridor space with display boards.'

Primary headteacher, Shropshire

Effective Learning Strategies

'We are an immersion learning environment!'

Primary headteacher, Renfrew, Scotland,
explaining why the times tables could be found
on the back of each cubicle door in the girls' toilets

Effective Learning Strategies

'Familiarize your class with alternative room layouts for learning. Make the floor plans visible. Your furniture moving teams operate on a rota and compete against the clock or with a timed piece of music. They learn to move the furniture for a different sort of learning.'

Effective Learning Strategies

'Research showed that a question is asked every 72 seconds; 38% of the questions are answered by the teachers themselves and, as pupils get older, their teachers talk more...'

Effective Questioning Strategies

LEADING
LEARNING

'In a while I'm going to ask what you already know about x. Before I do that, think of three things you already know about x... Now, when you are ready, describe your three things to your partner, then see if together you can get five things.'

Effective Questioning Strategies

Allow processing time so that the learner can:

* hear your question,
* assimilate it,
* formulate a response,
* and surface the response in language.

visit the website www.alite.co.uk

Effective Questioning Strategies

'The language of the average classroom is baffling to most pupils: avoid adult-based codes and put effort into describing what you want

not

what you don't want.'

Effective Questioning Strategies

Cue the learner
response by:

* pre-processing
* numbered challenge
* timed challenge
or
* structured challenge.

visit the website   www.alite.co.uk

Effective Questioning Strategies

'In a research project with 32 pupils from 11 infant and lower-junior classes, changing the teacher language in the classroom resulted in a 50% reduction in disruptive behaviour. Is your language simple, unambiguous, to the point and positive?'

Effective Questioning Strategies

'I try and deliver
the thinking skills in the
national curriculum,
by
the questions we ask
and by
the tasks I set.'

Secondary teacher, Kingston upon Hull, England

Effective Questioning Strategies

LEADING
LEARNING

'The best questions are the questions the learners ask for themselves.'

Effective Questioning Strategies

'Teaching pupils to identify similarities and differences and giving them the tools to do so, is an obvious shortcut to a thinking classroom.'

'The purpose
of a question
is for learning
to take place,
not testing
to take place.'

Bob Pike

'A key motivational question – how will I know I've done a really good job?'

Target Setting

'The only targets
which make
a difference
are those
we set
ourselves.'

Target Setting

'The target-setting mentality begins when we encourage outcomes-thinking in class.'

'The ability to set goals and work towards them marks the difference between success and failure.'

Target Setting

'Declare the goal, set achievable targets for the goal, break the targets into tasks, mark and give feedback on the tasks, revise the targets.'

Horsenden School's thoughts on bringing the targets to life:

* children use them daily

* they are visible in the classroom

* they are used as criteria for marking

* they are collectively celebrated when they are met

Horsenden School, Ealing

Target Setting

Factors enabling a school to target-set successfully:

*   the agreed aim is for students to take control of their learning
*   investment in training
*   an established assessment framework
*   the system is consistent even if staff change
*   staff are used to seeing, handling and analysing data
*   staff are used to using targets for planning and for focused teaching

Target Setting

'Teach the skills of target-setting in a neutral context and early, then use individual, group and class targets for motivation, purpose and feedback.'

Target Setting

'We use an academic monitoring programme where we try to get the pupil doing as much of the talking as possible. To do this we meet with the pupil termly and once a year with pupil and parents. The talk is all about targets and we take great care to practise by using the language of target-setting in everyday lessons.'

Deputy headteacher, Surrey

'If you want to
do target-setting then
do it well or not at all.
How do you do it well?
Give it time, give it
status.'

Target Setting

5 things that go wrong in target-setting:

* the focus is on quantity and presentation rather than learning
* students are involved too late or not at all
* over-emphasis on comparison with others
* staff and students don't understand purpose or worth
* feedback is for managerial or social purposes rather than learning

'Research suggests
that giving feedback
immediately after a test
is best, and that the
optimal time to test is
a day after the learning.'

Formative Assessment

'Development
and learning
are shaped
more by feedback
than
by input or
stimulus.'

'The best feedback is:

* in or near to the real experience

* authentic

* frequent

* removed from threat or sanction

* involving

* part of a learning cycle

...is yours?'

Formative Assessment

'In a 1994 review of 96 studies of motivation, it was found that overall, *reward does not decrease intrinsic motivation*. When interaction effects are examined, findings show that verbal praise produces an increase in intrinsic motivation. The only negative effect appears when expected tangible rewards are given to individuals for simply doing a task.'

Association for Supervision and Curriculum Development (ASCD), USA, September 2000

'A raw score on the page demotivates all but the high achievers; a raw score and comments and the vast majority do not even read your comments; educative feedback with bullet points for improvement is best.'

Black and Wiliam, *Inside the Black Box*, King's College, London, 1998

'To avoid the dread of yet another failure, break down the assessment criteria into very specific, very small and easily understood targets. Make the targets visible – put them up around the school! Then use these targets for marking and for motivation.'

Secondary teacher, London, England

Formative Assessment

'Over-reliance on crude grades demotivates even the best of learners.'

Formative Assessment

'I use a student assessment "conference" every term, where we all look at the criteria for grading again and then set about assessing each other's work.'

Teacher, Cornwall, England

Formative Assessment

'There are strong correlations between performance in teacher tests and performance in external tests, often because they measure the same thing: the ability to do well in tests.

There has to be more to learning in a knowledge age than doing well in tests.'

Formative Assessment

'In a 1992 review of 7,827 studies in education, Hattle found that accurate and detailed feedback to students can increase their level of knowledge and understanding by 37 percentile points.'

Association for Supervision and Curriculum Development (ASCD), USA, September 2000

Formative Assessment

'The validity of student self-assessment is sometimes questioned. In our experience students commonly demonstrate a clear-headed capacity to evaluate their own work.'

L Darling-Hammond et al., *Authentic Assessment in Action,* New York: Teachers College Press, © 1995 by Teachers College, Columbia University

LEADING
LEARNING

5 factors for improving pupils' learning through assessment:

*   provision of effective feedback to pupils
*   active involvement of pupils
*   adjustments to teaching
*   motivation and self-esteem via assessment
*   pupils' self-assessment in order to understand how to improve

Black and Wiliam, *Inside the Black Box*, King's College, London, 1998

visit the website www.alite.co.uk

'Many students run in fear of self-testing because they are frightened of finding out the results, and because teachers don't allow them to practise it. This is ironic because it is a skill which is at the core of independent learning.'

'Self-test spells success.'

'More frequent tests in classrooms, not fewer, but make those tests varied, informal and rich in feedback.'

'Neurological trials support the notion of "little and often" being better than a binge. Don't leave it too late to revise.'

10 arguments for mock exams:

1. They provide a significant milestone in a two-year course.

2. They ensure that the majority of teaching is completed ahead of time.

3. They identify borderline candidates.

4. They give authentic practice of exam technique.

5. Revision programmes can be structured from the data gathered.

6. They confirm tier entry decisions.

7. Candidates get to rehearse exam preparation.

8. They provide the best material for review.

9. They provide comparative data.

10. They allow you to collect information about candidates' strengths and weaknesses.

'To help pupils improve exam performance use the "steps" model of % point improvements at a time towards the next grade.'

'In the English department we have an "8 steps to heaven" week. This is when we look at 8 different % point improvements that pupils can make a % at a time. We give all 8 suggestions on a checklist which says "are you doing this?" and they go through all their work individually then in co-operative pairs.'

Head of English, Leeds

'We display the working at grades for KS4. These attract a great deal of attention because they record where students are currently performing and what their % improvement over the previous half-term has been. They know that in order to get on the year trip to the theme park they have to accumulate performance or performance improvement points.'

Deputy headteacher, Birmingham

Preparing for Exams

'Teach the skills of mental rehearsal of success and relaxation in the context of exams. Get them to run a movie in their heads of successfully using good exam technique and run that movie again and again so that it comes naturally to them when it's for real...'

Preparing for Exams

4 essentials for exam preparation:

* distributed testing
* exam technique
* mental rehearsal
* authentic practice

5 ways to develop a thinking classroom:

* pole-bridging

* learning coaching

* processing cues

* structured pair-shares

* the question generator

Thinking Skills

'Metacognition is the ability to monitor one's own pattern of thought and habits of mind. It is metacognition which makes us human.'

LEADING LEARNING

'We do not think in a linear, sequential way, yet every body of information is given to us in a linear manner. Every language structure is basically linear... we are taught to communicate in a way that is actually restricting our ability to think.'

Richard Saul Wurmann,
Information Anxiety, Pan, 1991

Thinking Skills

'Metacognition –
thinking about thinking
– can be modelled and
taught in any lesson,
and is a skill which
is genuinely
life transforming.'

Thinking Skills

'Without any shadow of a doubt, the best way to develop the "skills" of "thinking" is to do so within and through the immersion of real and sustained learning challenge.'

Thinking Skills

'When you map your understanding, you actively seek patterns, hierarchies, similarities and differences.
You aggregate up and dis-aggregate down: this is inking thinking!'

Thinking Skills

'When we think, we are capable of processing 1,200–1,600 words each minute; when we write we can, at best, manage 25–35 words each minute: which skill should we develop?'

Thinking Skills

'Teaching thinking...
is not an
alternative
to the standards
agenda but a way of
taking it forward.'

Professor Michael Barber,
UK government education adviser

Thinking Skills

'Is this
a
thinking
lesson,
sir?'

Thinking Skills

LEADING LEARNING

'Save yourselves some money. Invest in quality staff development which helps teachers structure variety in their questioning and in their design of open-ended problem-solving activities.
Use protocols – for language exchange and group interaction directed to task. Avoid buying any "thinking skills" solution off the shelf!'

Thinking Skills

'But what if intelligence could be taught?'

Models of Intelligence

'If anything, the essence of intelligence would seem to be in knowing when to act quickly, and knowing when to think and act slowly.'

Professor Robert Sternberg

Models of Intelligence

'Ultimately, a full understanding of any concept of any complexity cannot be restricted to a single mode of knowing.'

Howard Gardner, Professor of Education and Adjunct Professor of Neuroscience, Harvard

Models of Intelligence

Gardner's 'multiple' intelligences:

* mathematical/logical

* linguistic

* visual/spatial

* kinesthetic

* intrapersonal

* interpersonal

* musical

* naturalist

* (existential/spiritual)

'Brain areas can change in size and function over a number of days.'

Models of Intelligence

'Our reward system is based on multiple intelligence. We want to recognize different sorts of talents. We use a baccalaureate system of gold, silver and bronze and look for the best examples across the eight different intelligences.'

Deputy headteacher, secondary school, Essex

Models of Intelligence

'I've yet to meet a successful dentist, airline pilot or professional golfer who did not possess kinesthetic intelligence to a significant degree. The ability to manoeuvre your body in skilful ways pays you handsomely.'

'Persistence is the number one intelligent behaviour and it can be modelled and taught.'

'Managing the moment of impulsivity is at the heart of an intelligent response. Developing the skill of knowing when it is appropriate to act quickly, and when it is more appropriate to think and act slowly, prepares you for life.'

'Information

is not

knowledge.'

Susan Greenfield, Professor of Pharmacology and
Director of the Royal Institution

Models of Intelligence

Some differences to consider:

* leading vs managing

* important vs urgent

* learning vs teaching

* recall vs recognition

* relevant vs irrelevant

* effective vs efficient

* cause vs effect

* principles vs techniques

* striding vs strolling

'You are the lead learner in your own classroom.'

Staff Development

LEADING
LEARNING

'The most effective leaders can change the culture of the school by understanding the classroom conditions in which improvement can take place. They need to develop a capacity in their staff for continuing professional development and a continuing dialogue with them on teaching methods and classroom organization.'

Professor David Hopkins,
School Improvement for Real 2001,
Falmer Press

Staff Development

'There is more variation within schools than between schools and the biggest area of difference is in the quality of the learning experience: what are you doing about it?'

Staff Development

LEADING
LEARNING

Learning has not occurred until behaviours change:

I was...

I am...

I will be...

Staff Development

The most effective form of staff development is coaching on the job. So more:

* programmes, fewer events
* action research
* learning research groups
* internal secondments
* mentoring
* school-wide protocols around learning
* structured peer-observation
* quality, extended induction
* external accreditation
* alignment with strategic planning

Learning has not occurred until behaviours change.

As a result of this experience:

I will now...
*
*
*

and I would like my department to...
*
*
*

and I would like the school to...
*
*
*

Staff Development

10 suggestions for schools using these posters

1. Display in staffrooms and in faculty offices.
2. Use the topic on the poster as a focus for the week or fortnight and then review as part of a staff briefing or departmental meeting.
3. Use as prompts for discussion and debate as part of staff development. Have copies available for departmental INSET and in the staff development library.
4. Use the posters to stimulate further ideas and strategies for effective teaching – for example, ten ways to start a lesson positively.
5. Use a selection as screen savers on the school computer network or as thought for the week in the staff bulletin or on the school cctv.
6. Use as teaching tools and provide excerpts in the staff handbook.
7. New and newly qualified staff could access a selection as part of the induction programme.
8. Adapt a selection for presentations to parents on how to help your child learn.
9. Put on the school website as a staff development resource.
10. Use as a focus for action research within the school.